VOCAL/PIANO

JACKIE EVANCHO

SONGS FROM
THE SILVER SCREEN

ISBN 978-1-4803-0862-6

7777 W. BLUEMOUND RD. P.O. BOX 13819 MILWAUKEE, WI 53213

Visit Hal Leonard Online at
www.halleonard.com

4   PURE IMAGINATION

12   THE MUSIC OF THE NIGHT

17   CAN YOU FEEL THE LOVE TONIGHT

22   REFLECTION

29   THE SUMMER KNOWS

34   I SEE THE LIGHT

43   WHAT A WONDERFUL WORLD

49   SE

53   MY HEART WILL GO ON

61   COME WHAT MAY

69   SOME ENCHANTED EVENING

75   WHEN I FALL IN LOVE

PURE IMAGINATION
from WILLY WONKA AND THE CHOCOLATE FACTORY

Words and Music by LESLIE BRICUSSE
and ANTHONY NEWLEY

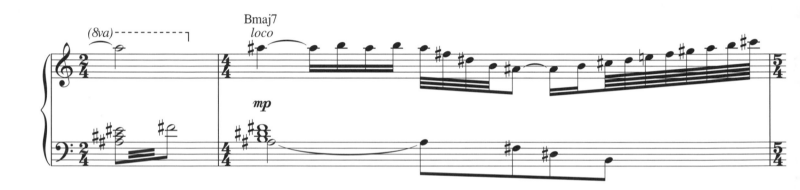

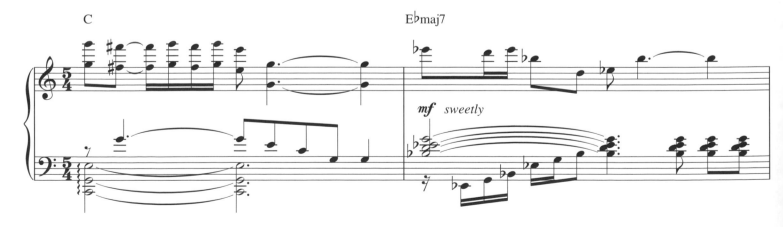

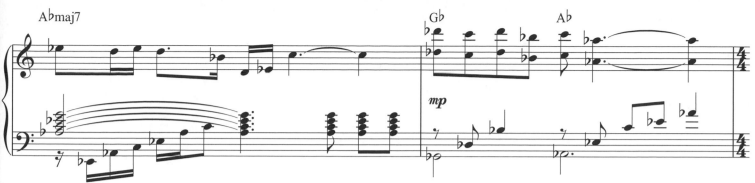

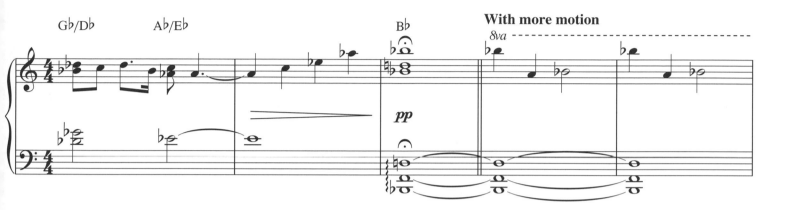

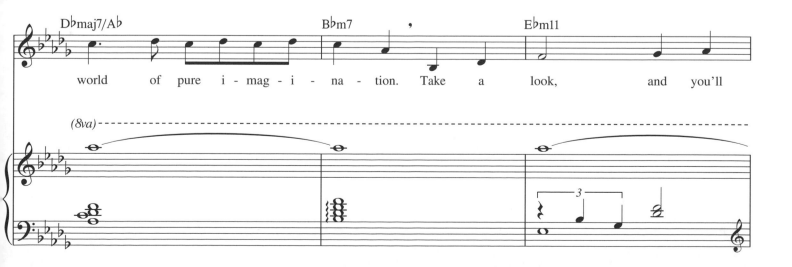

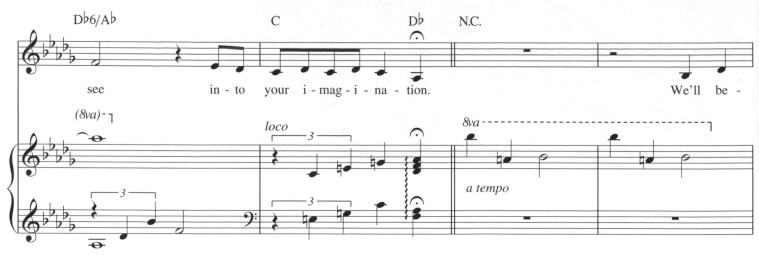

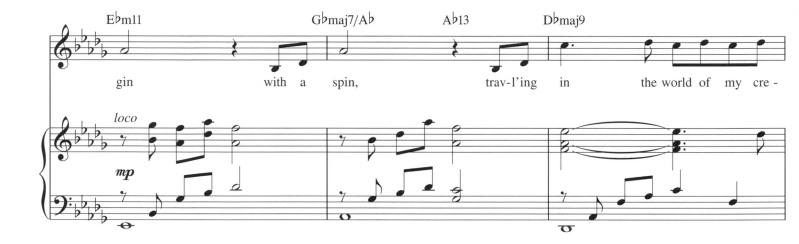

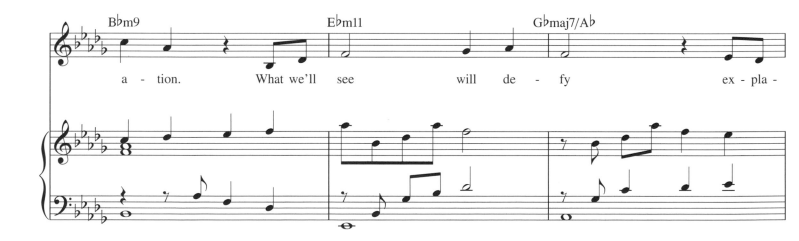

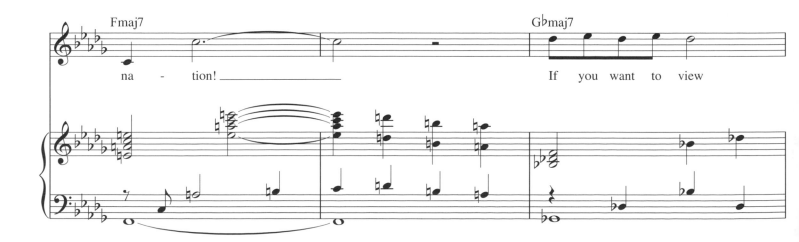

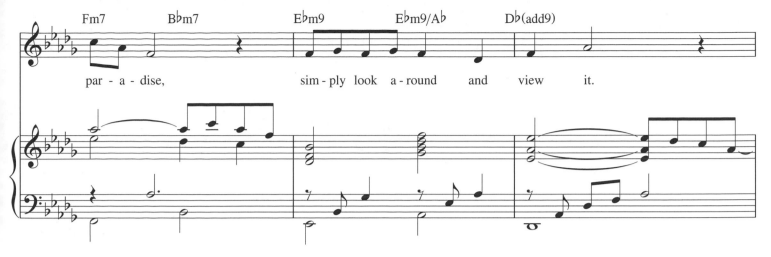

par - a - dise,   sim - ply look a - round   and   view   it.

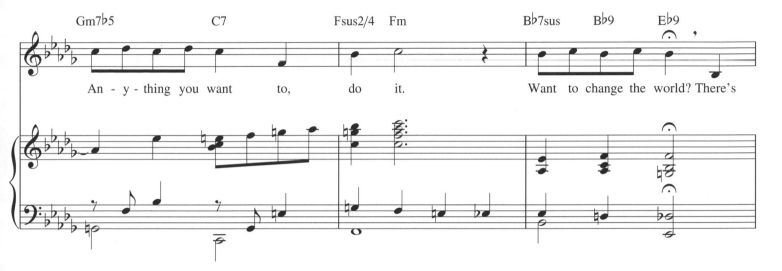

An - y - thing you want   to,   do   it.   Want to change the world? There's

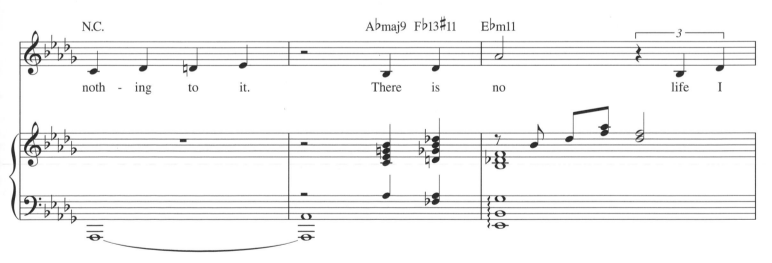

noth - ing to it.   There   is   no   life   I

know   to com - pare   with pure i - mag - i - na - tion. Liv - ing

there, you'll be free, if you tru - ly

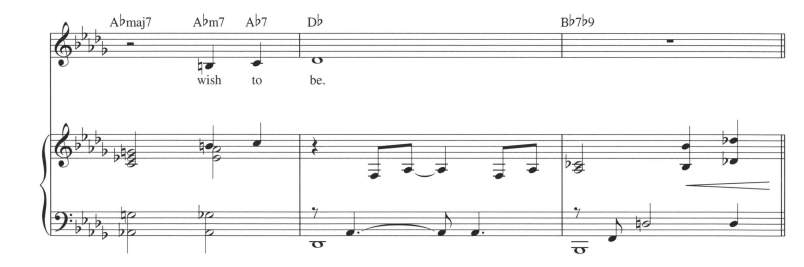

wish to be.

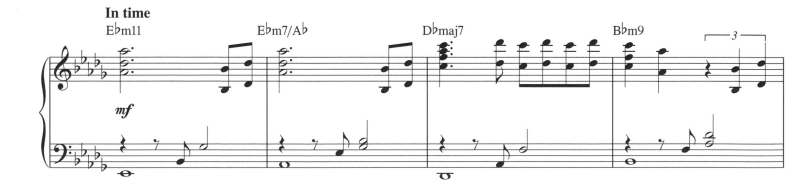

In time

na - tion. Take a look, and you'll see in - to

your i - mag - i - na - tion. _____ There is no _____ life I

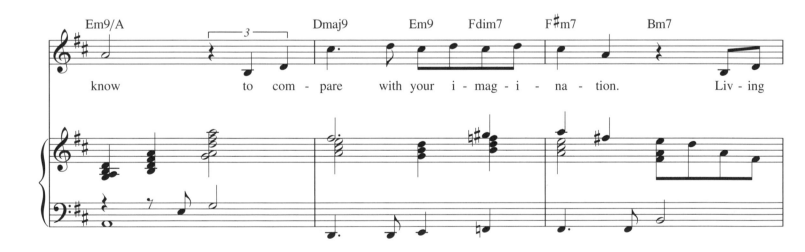

know to com - pare with your i - mag - i - na - tion. Liv - ing

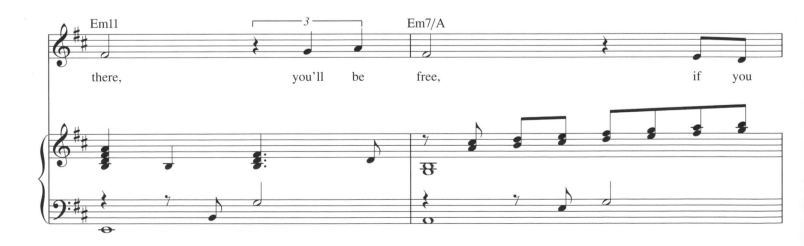

there, you'll be free, if you

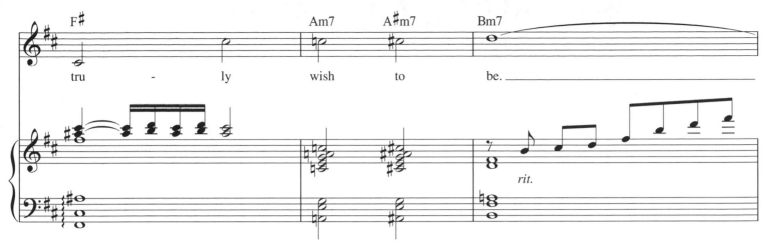

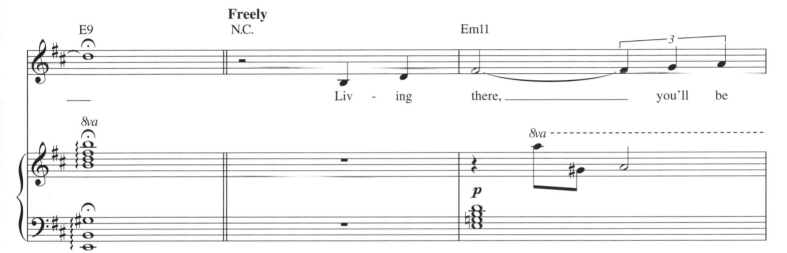

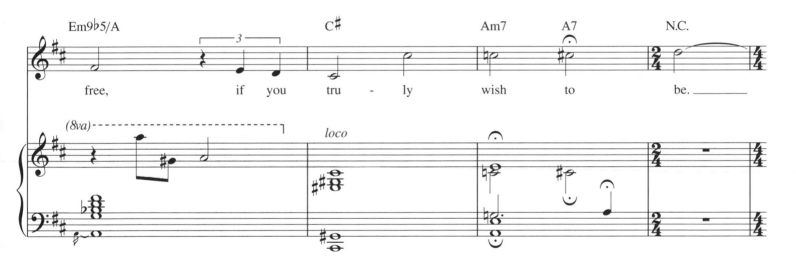

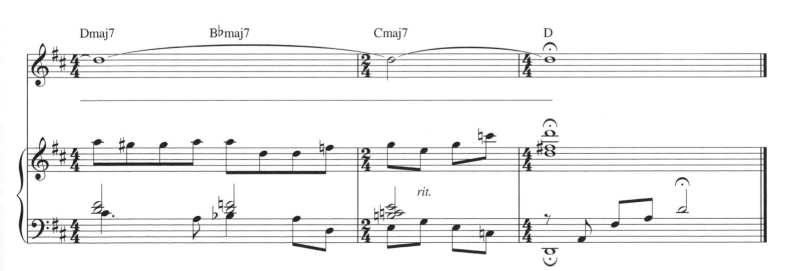

THE MUSIC OF THE NIGHT
from THE PHANTOM OF THE OPERA

Music by ANDREW LLOYD WEBBER
Lyrics by CHARLES HART
Additional Lyrics by RICHARD STILGOE

thoughts of the life you knew be - fore. Close your
thoughts of the life you knew be - fore. Let your

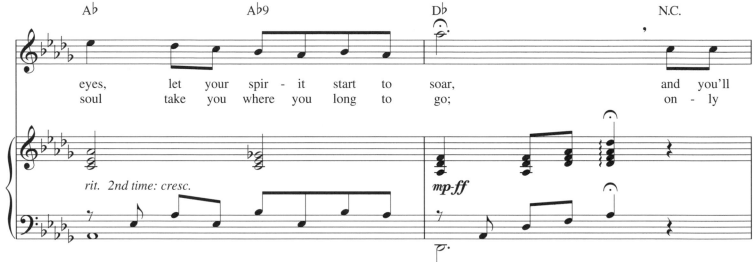

eyes, let your spir - it start to soar, and you'll
soul take you where you long to go; on - ly

rit. 2nd time: cresc.

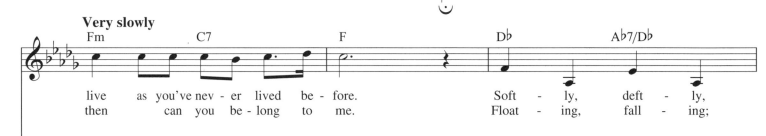

Very slowly

live as you've nev - er lived be - fore. Soft - ly, deft - ly,
then can you be - long to me. Float - ing, fall - ing;

a tempo

mu - sic shall ca - ress you. Hear it, feel it
sweet in - tox - i - ca - tion! Touch me, trust me;

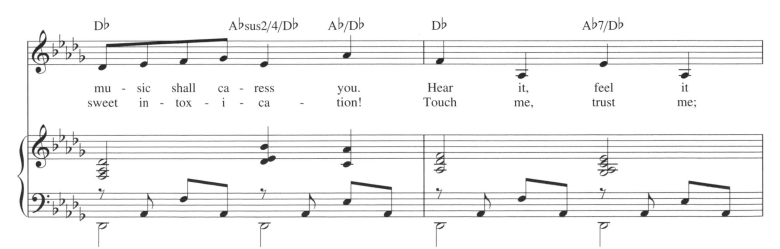

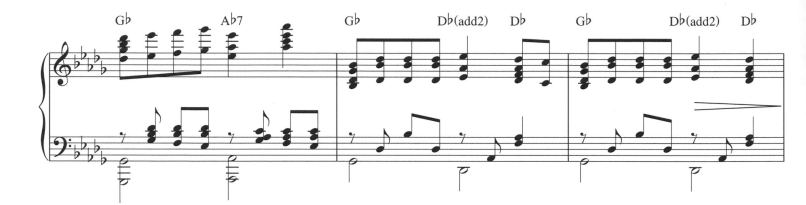

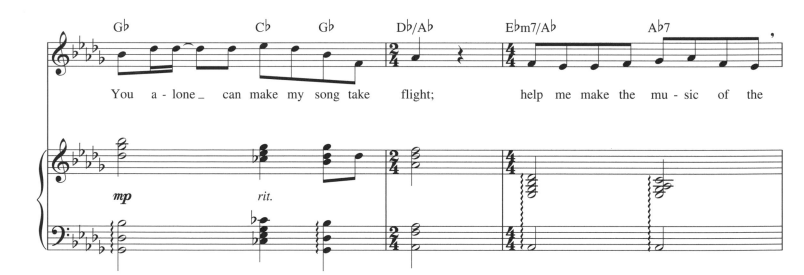

You a - lone _ can make my song take flight; help me make the mu - sic of the

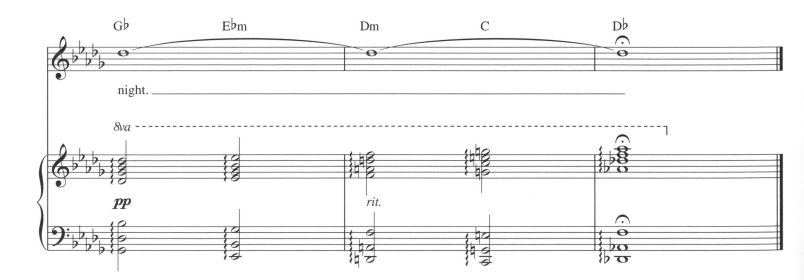

night. _____

CAN YOU FEEL THE LOVE TONIGHT

from Walt Disney Pictures' THE LION KING

Music by ELTON JOHN
Lyrics by TIM RICE

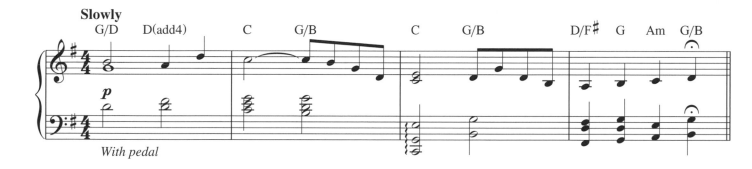

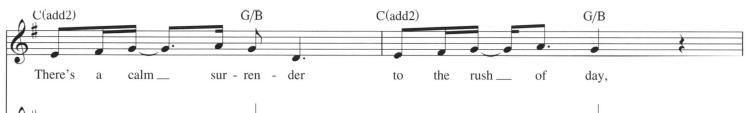

There's a calm ___ sur-ren-der to the rush ___ of day,

when the heat ___ of a roll-ing wind can be turned ___ a-way. ___

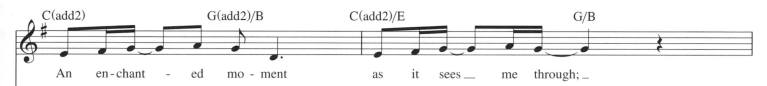

An en-chant-ed mo-ment as it sees ___ me through; ___

it's e - nough _ for this rest - less war - rior just to be _ with you. _ And

can you feel _ the love _ to - night? _ It is where we

are. It's e - nough _ for this

wide - eyed wan - der - er that we got this far. _

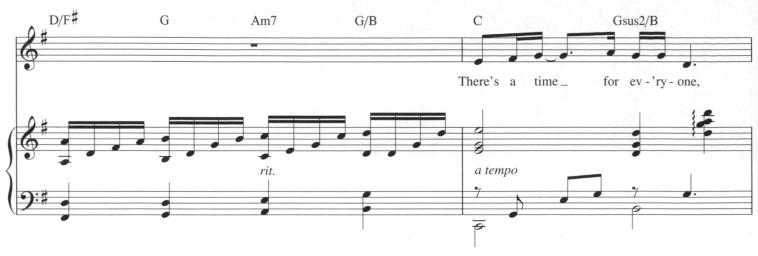

REFLECTION
from Walt Disney Pictures' MULAN

Music by MATTHEW WILDER
Lyrics by DAVID ZIPPEL

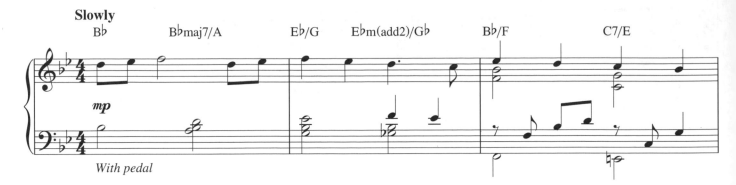

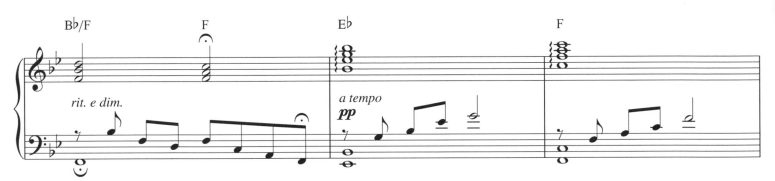

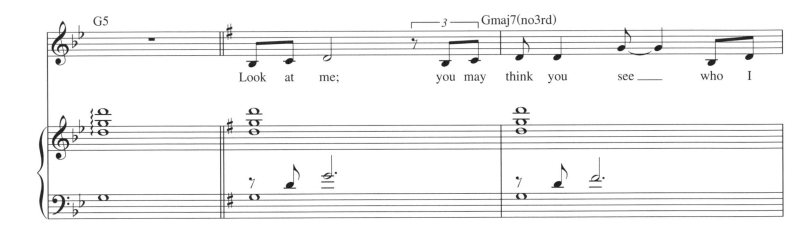

Look at me; you may think you see ___ who I

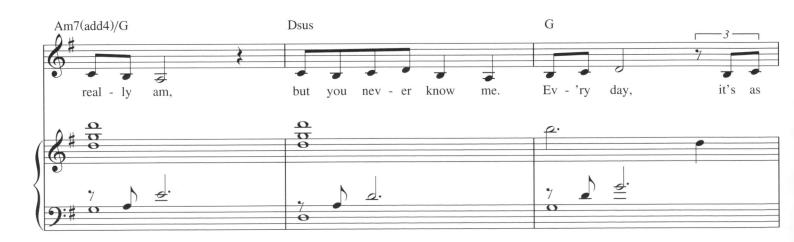

real - ly am, but you nev - er know me. Ev - 'ry day, it's as

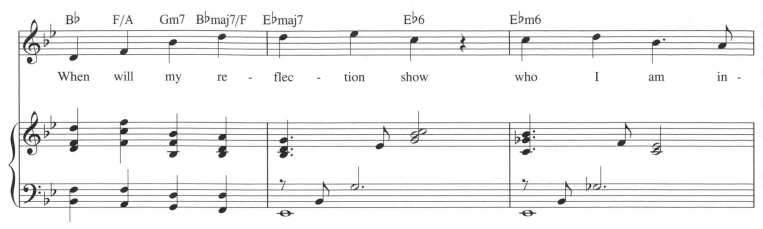

When will my re - flec - tion show who I am in -

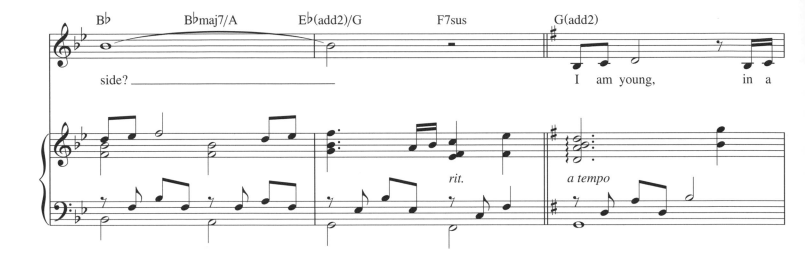

side? _____ I am young, in a

world where I ___ have to hide my heart ___ and what I be - lieve in.

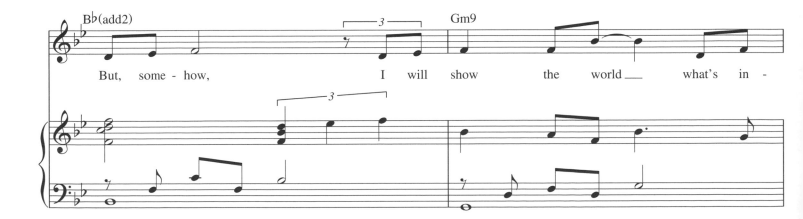

But, some - how, I will show the world ___ what's in -

side my heart, _ and be loved for who I ___ am. ___

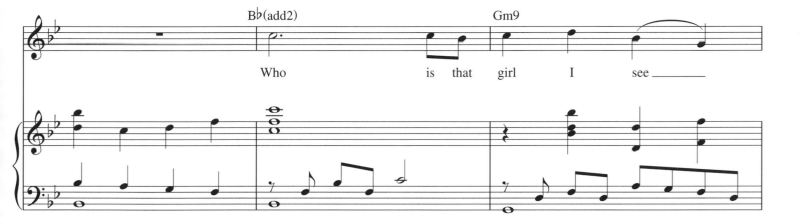

Who is that girl I see _____

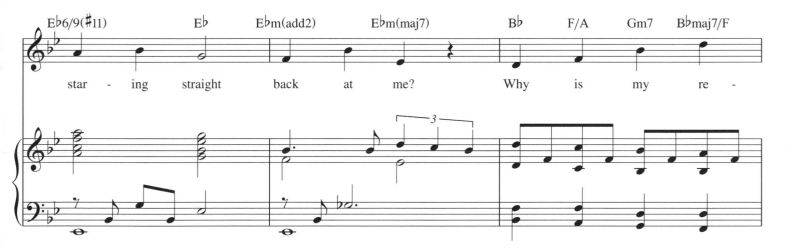

star - ing straight back at me? Why is my re -

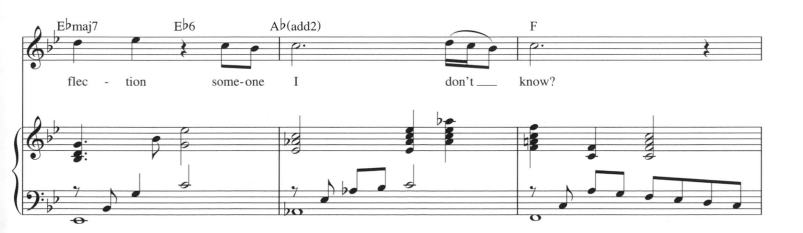

flec - tion some-one I don't ___ know?

Must I pre-tend that I'm _____ some-one else

for all time? When will my re-flec-tion show

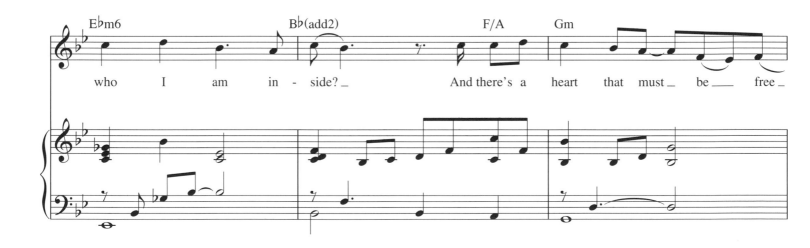

who I am in-side? _ And there's a heart that must_ be _____ free _

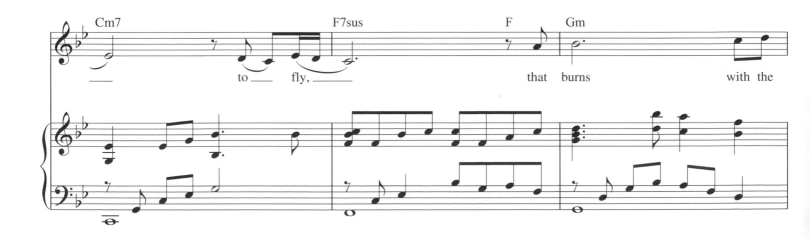

to _____ fly, _____ that burns with the

need to know _ the rea - son why. _____

Why must we all con - ceal what we think,
I won't pre - tend that I'm some - one else

how we feel? Must there be a sim - pler me I'm
for all time. When will my re - flec - tion show

forced to ___ hide?   who I am in -

side? _____

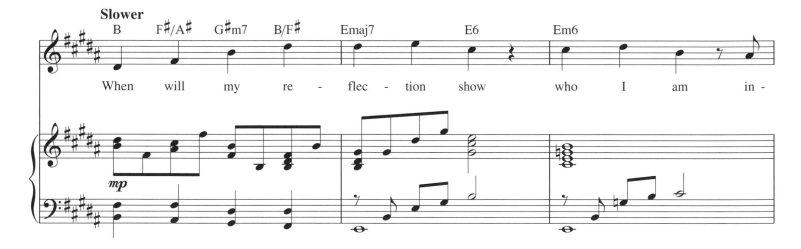

Slower

When will my re - flec - tion show   who I am in -

side? _____

rit. e dim.

THE SUMMER KNOWS
Theme from SUMMER OF '42

Lyrics by ALAN and MARILYN BERGMAN
Music by MICHEL LEGRAND

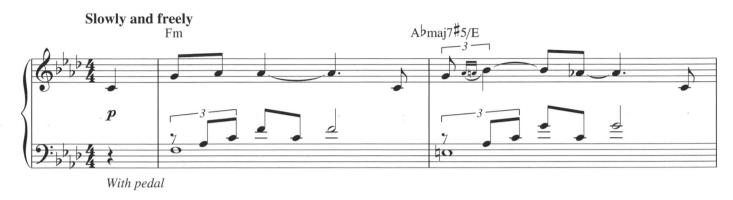

The sum-mer smiles, the sum-mer knows; and,

un - a - shamed, _ she sheds her clothes. The

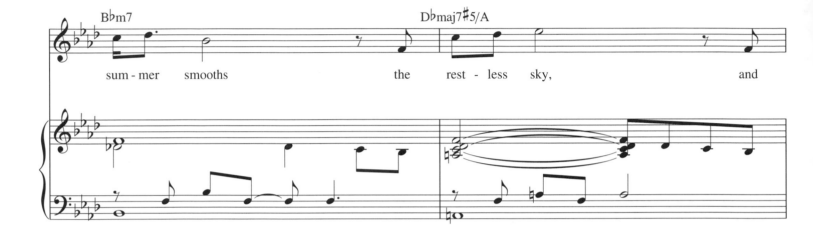

sum - mer smooths the rest - less sky, and

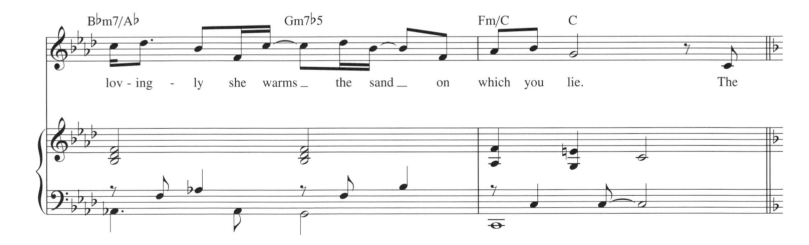

lov - ing - ly she warms _ the sand _ on which you lie. The

With more motion

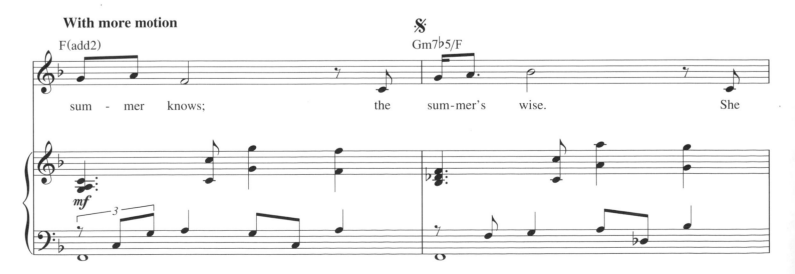

sum - mer knows; the sum-mer's wise. She

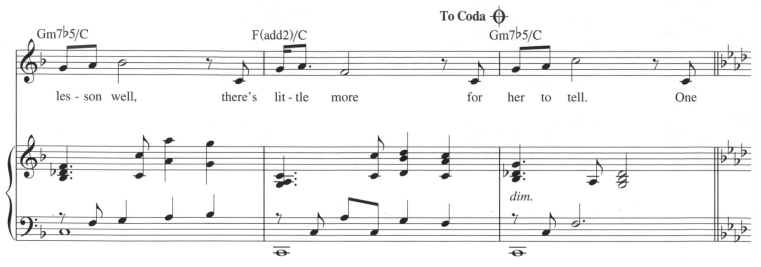

les-son well, there's lit-tle more for her to tell. One

A little slower

last ca-ress;__ it's time to dress for fall.

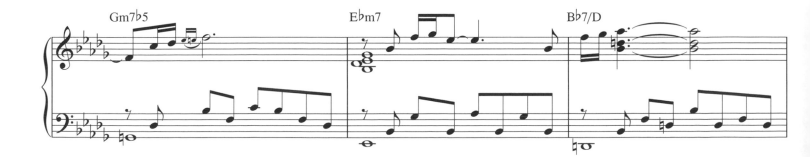

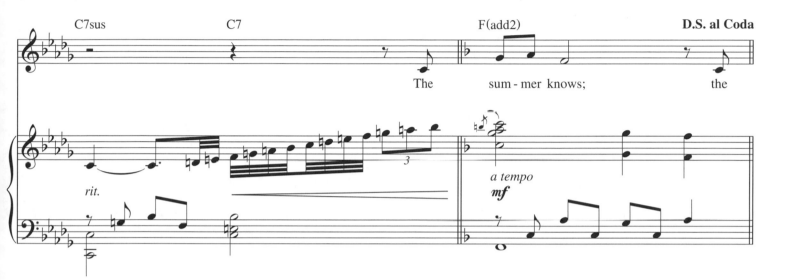

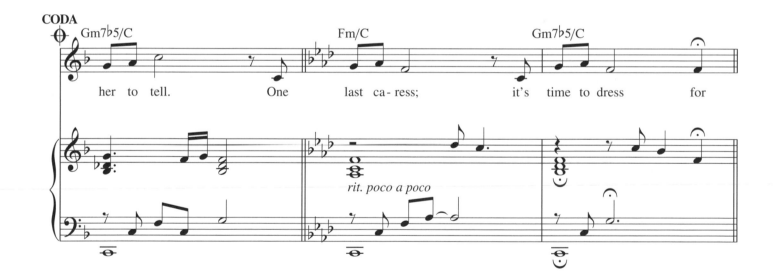

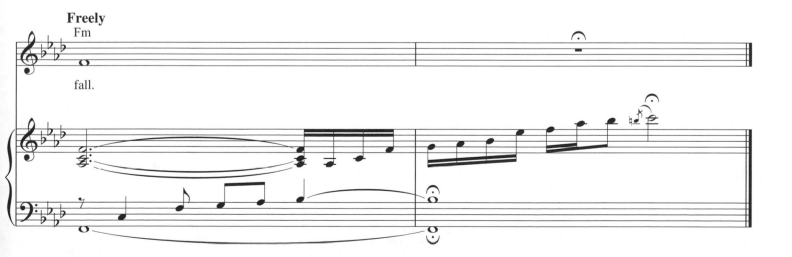

I SEE THE LIGHT

from Walt Disney Pictures' TANGLED

Music by ALAN MENKEN
Lyrics by GLENN SLATER

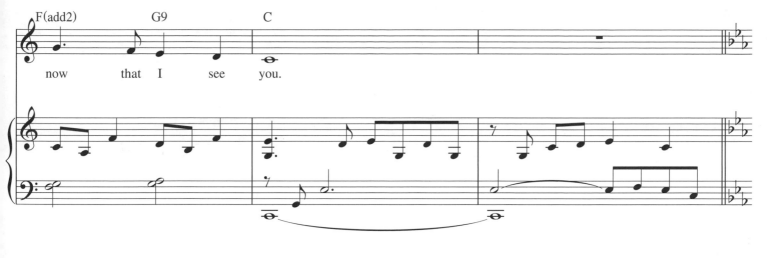

now　　that I　see　you.

Male lead: All those days chas - ing＿ down a day - dream;

all those years liv - ing＿ in a blur.

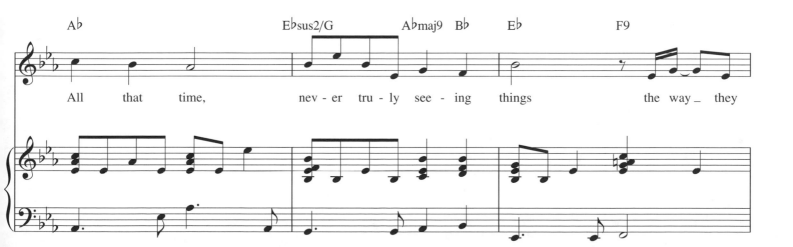

All that time, nev - er tru - ly see - ing things the way＿ they

were.   Now she's here, shin - ing in the star- light.

Now she's here; sud - den - ly, _____ I know:

if she's here, it's crys - tal clear; I'm where I'm meant to

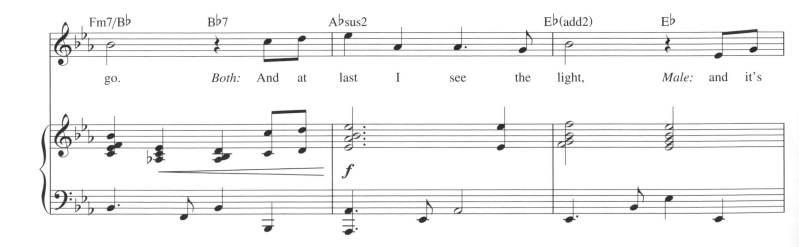

go. *Both:* And at last I see the light, *Male:* and it's

A little slower

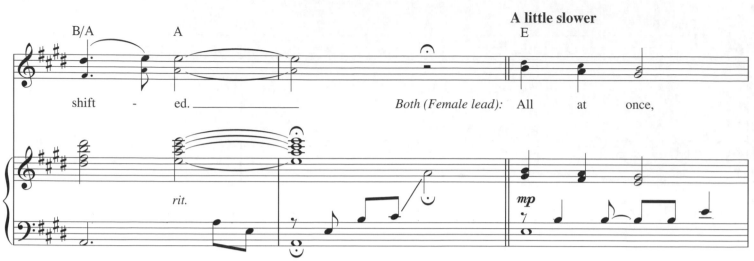

shift - ed. _____ *Both (Female lead):* All at once,

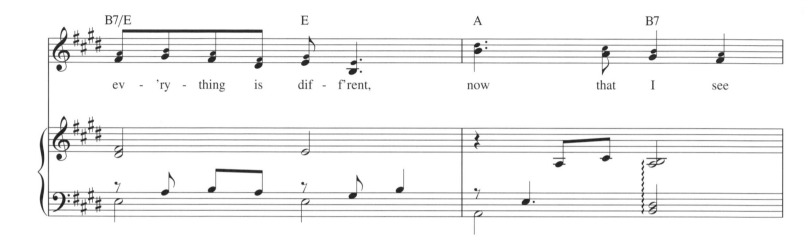

ev - 'ry - thing is dif - f'rent, now that I see

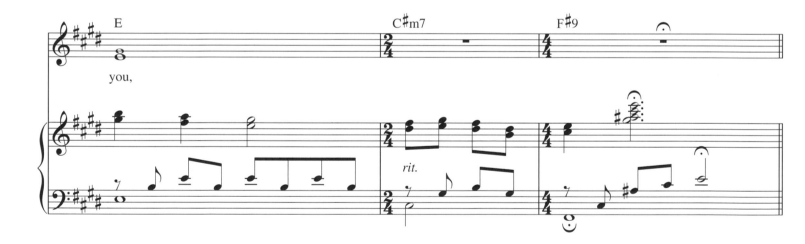

you,

Freely

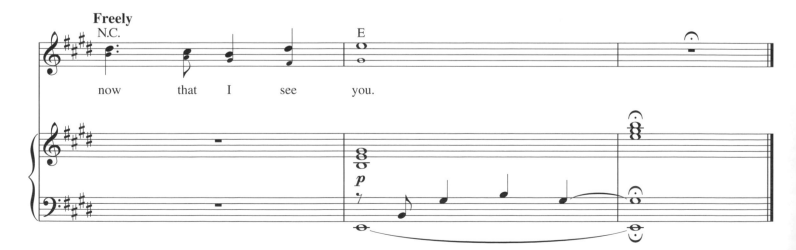

now that I see you.

WHAT A WONDERFUL WORLD
featured in the Motion Picture GOOD MORNING VIETNAM

Words and Music by GEORGE DAVID WEISS
and BOB THIELE

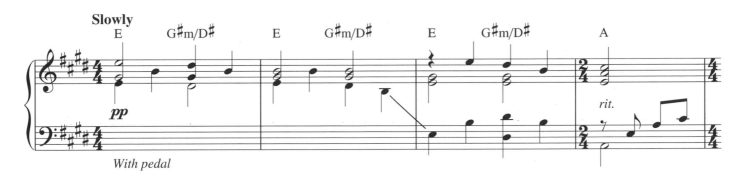

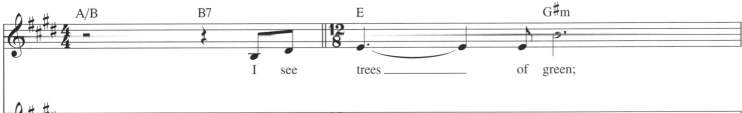

"What a won - der - ful world." I ___ see

skies _____ of blue and clouds of white; the

bright bless - ed day, the dark _____ sa - cred night. And I

think to __ my - self, "What a won - der - ful world."

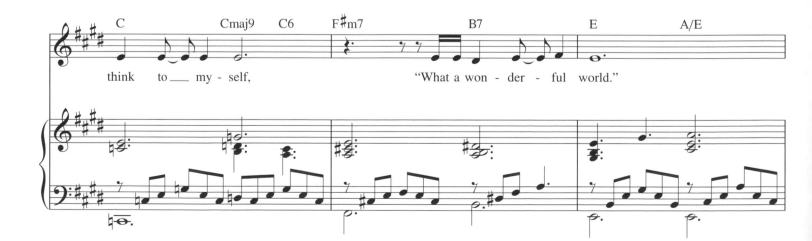

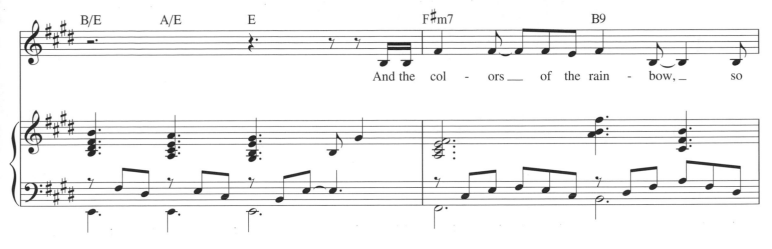

And the col - ors __ of the rain - bow, __ so

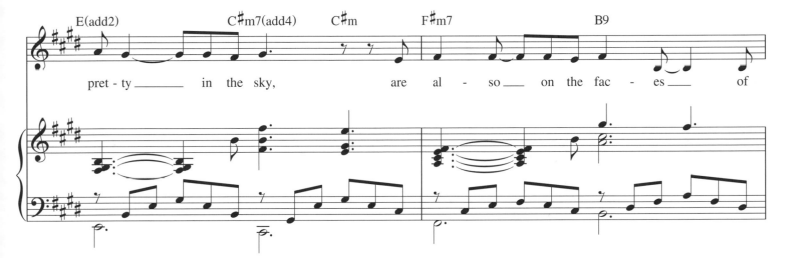

pret - ty __ in the sky, are al - so __ on the fac - es __ of

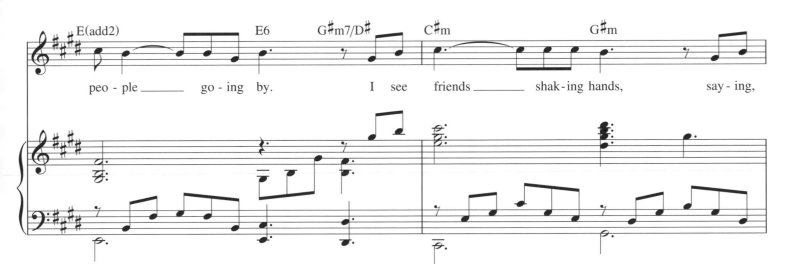

peo - ple __ go - ing by. I see friends __ shak - ing hands, say - ing,

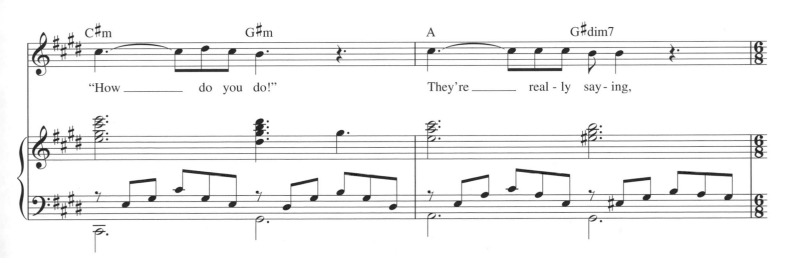

"How __ do you do!" They're __ real - ly say - ing,

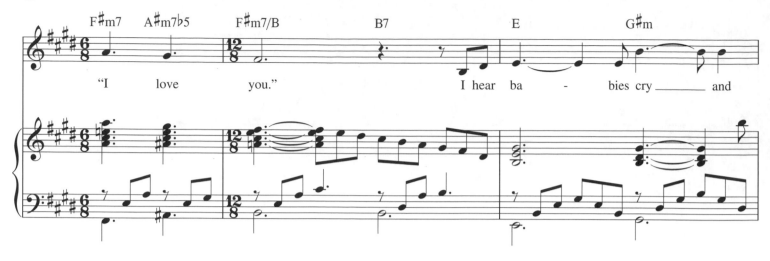

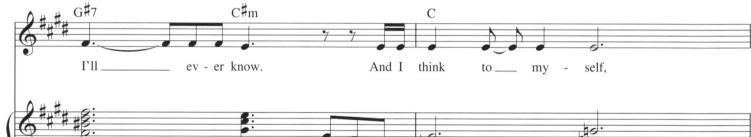

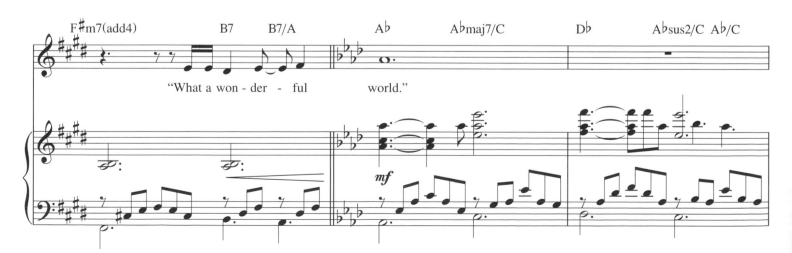

SE
from CINEMA PARADISO

Written by ANDREA MORRICONE
and ENNICIO MORRICONE

Se _____ tu fos - si nei miei
Sc _____ tu fos - si nel mio

oc - chi per un gior - no,   ve - dres - ti la bel - lez - za   che,
cuo - re per un gior - no,   po - tres - te a - ve - re u - n'i - de - a   di

pie - na d'al - le - gri - a,   lo tro - vo den - tro gli oc - chi
ciò che sen - to i - o   quan - do m'ab - brac - ci for - te a

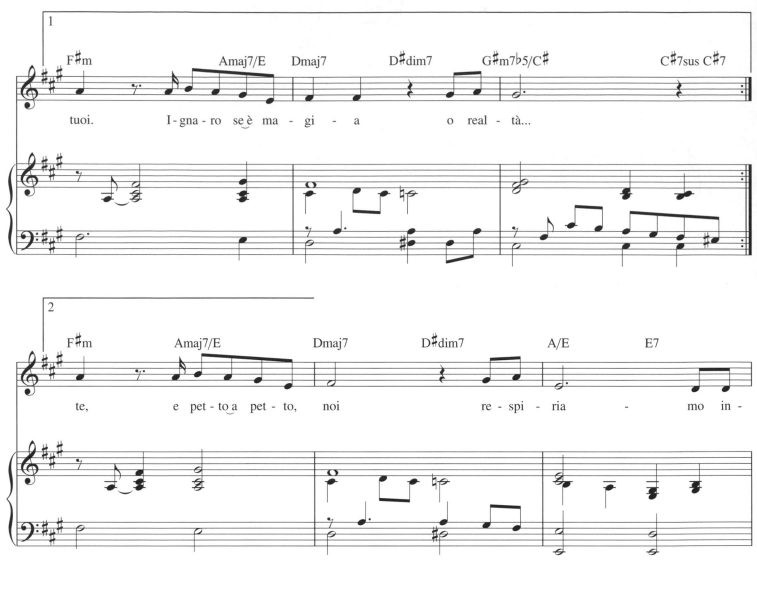

tuoi. I - gna - ro se è ma - gi - a o real - tà...

te, e pet - to a pet - to, noi re - spi - ria - mo in -

sie - me.

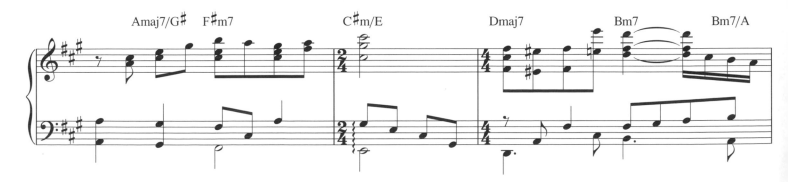

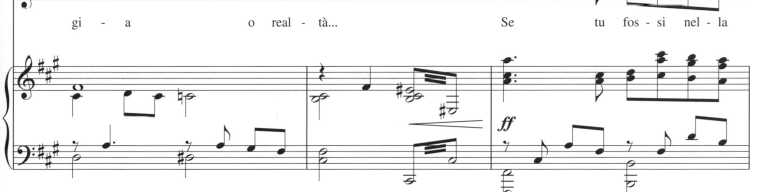

MY HEART WILL GO ON
(Love Theme From 'Titanic')
from the Paramount and Twentieth Century Fox Motion Picture TITANIC

Music by JAMES HORNER
Lyric by WILL JENNINGS

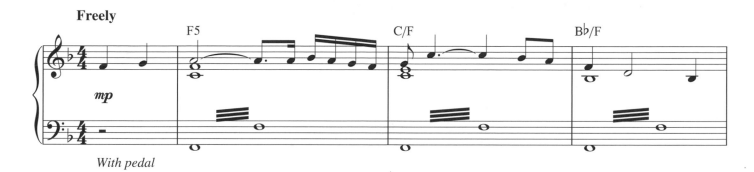

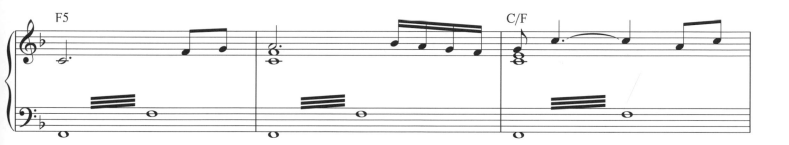

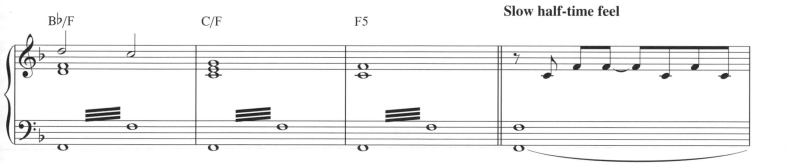

see you,   I feel   you;   that   is how   I

know   you   go   on. _____

Far   a - cross   the   dis - tance   and   spac - es   be -

tween   us,   you   have come   to   show   you   go

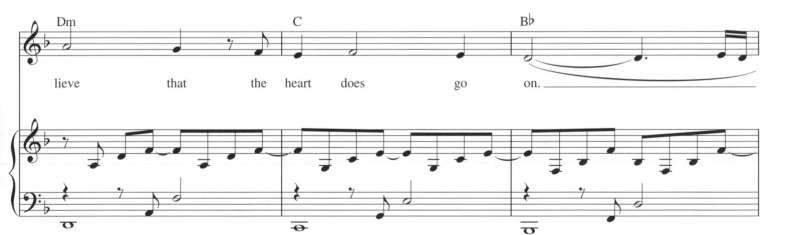

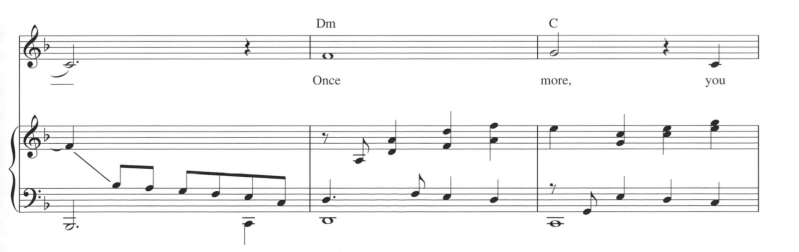

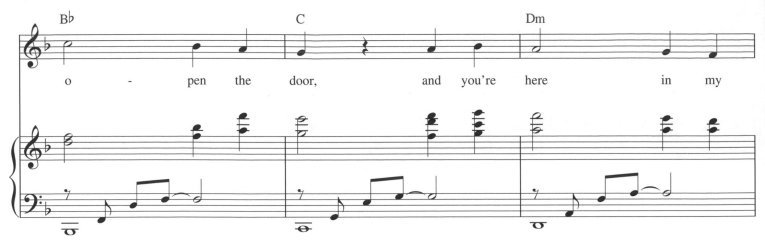

o - pen the door, and you're here in my

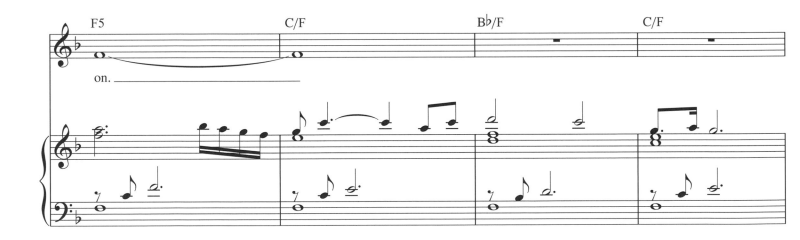

heart, and my heart will go on _____ and

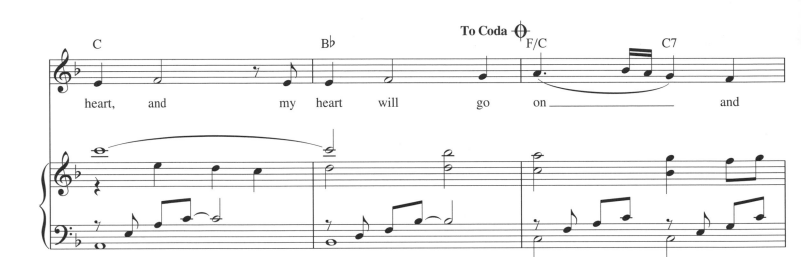

on. _____

Love can touch us one time and last for a

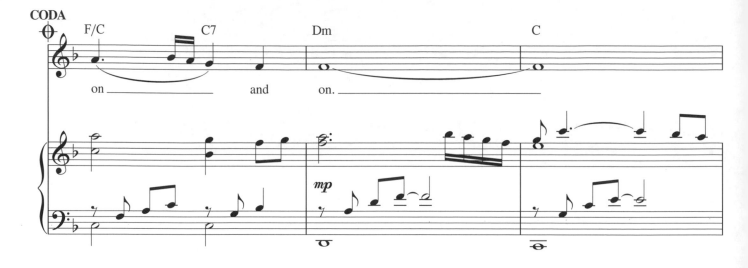

on _____ and on. _____

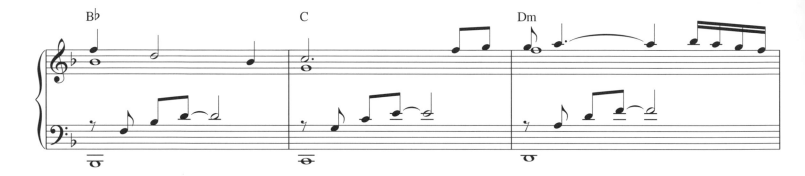

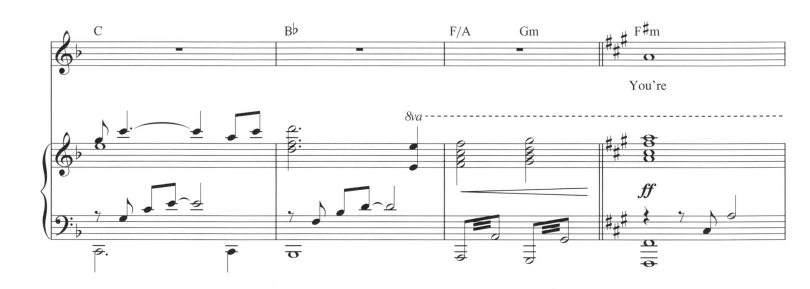

You're

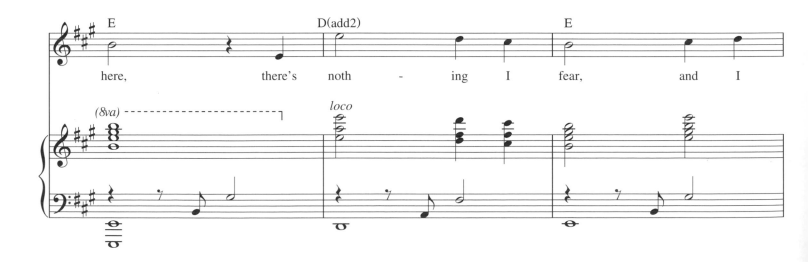

here,   there's   noth - ing   I   fear,   and   I

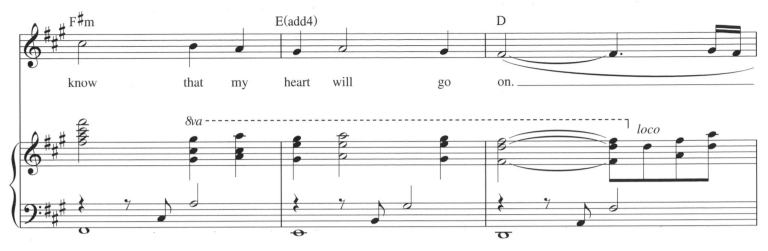

know that my heart will go on.

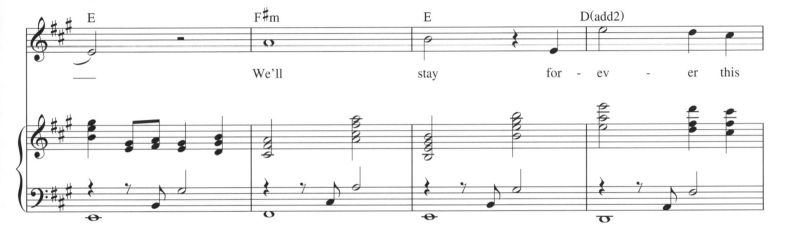

We'll stay for - ev - er this

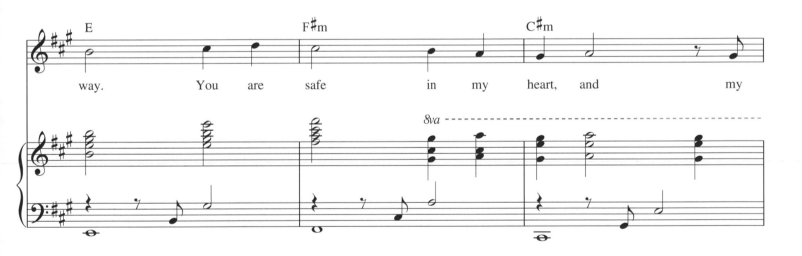

way. You are safe in my heart, and my

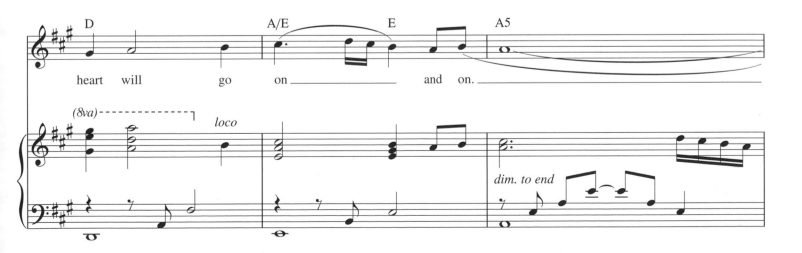

heart will go on and on.

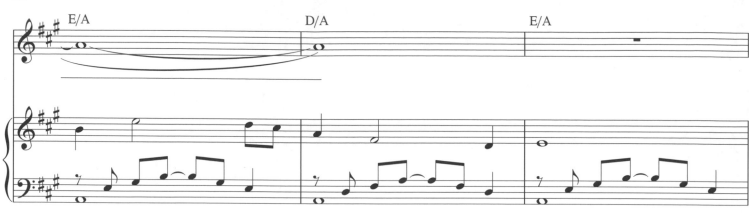

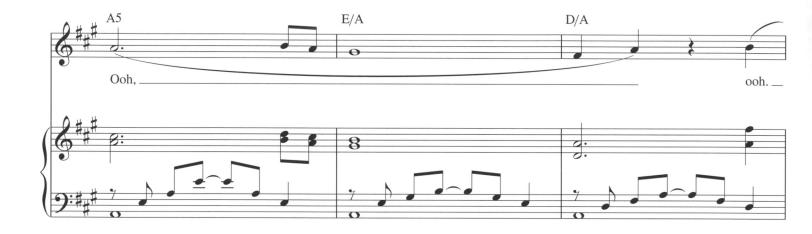

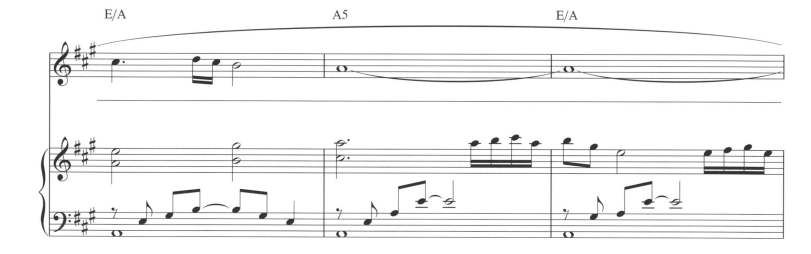

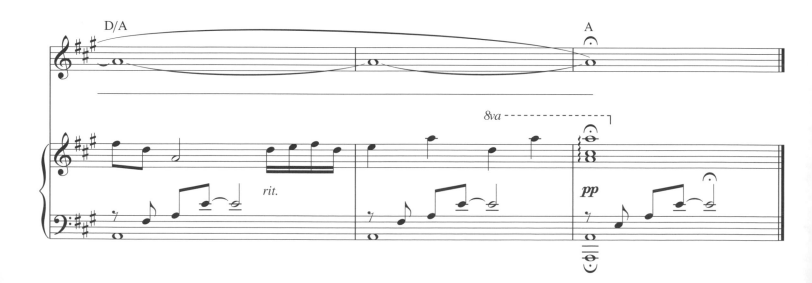

COME WHAT MAY
from the Motion Picture MOULIN ROUGE

Words and Music by
DAVID BAERWALD

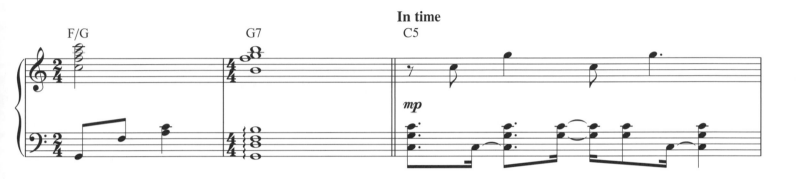

Female vocal: Nev - er knew I could ___ feel like this,

like I've __ nev - er seen __ the sky be - fore.

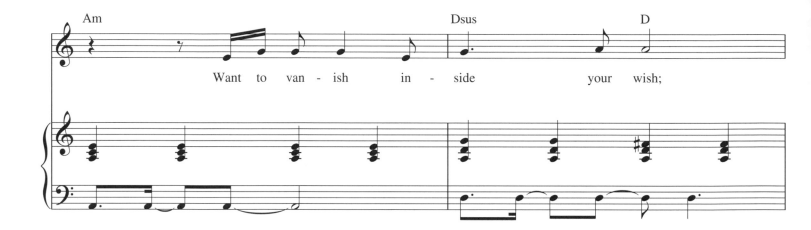

Want to van - ish in - side your wish;

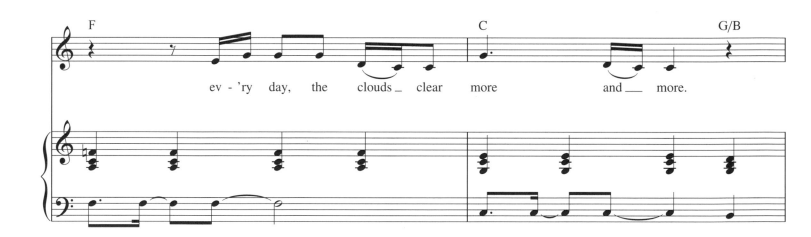

ev - 'ry day, the clouds __ clear more and __ more.

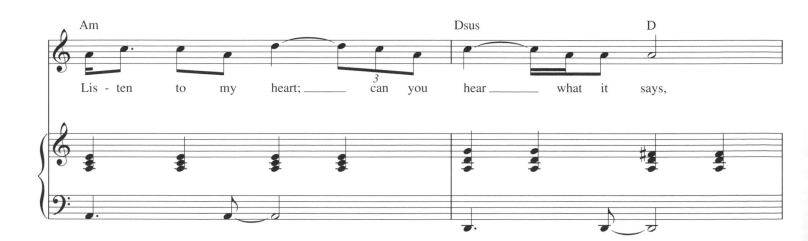

Lis - ten to my heart; __ can you hear _____ what it says,

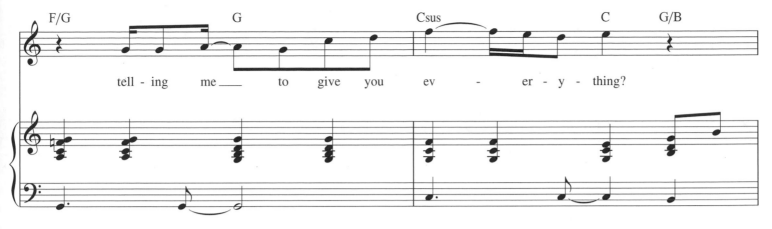

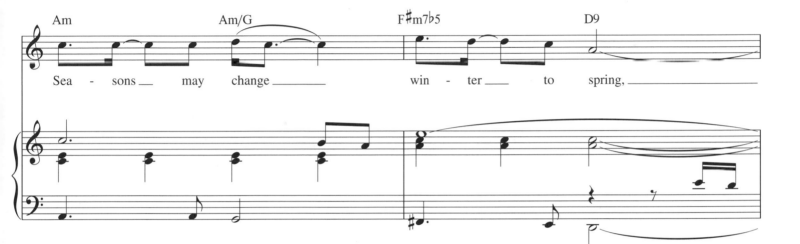

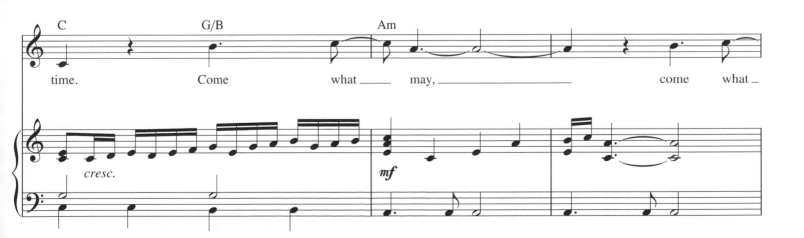

may, _____ I will love you un - til my

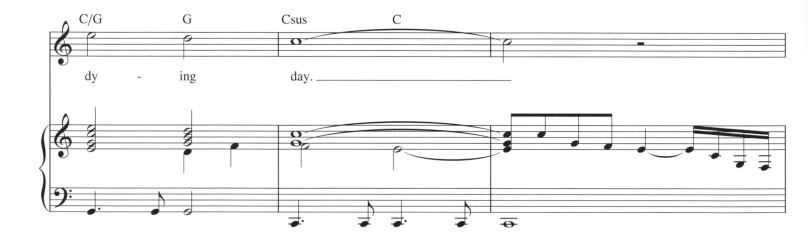

dy - ing day. _____

Male vocal: Sud - den - ly the world seems such a per - fect place;

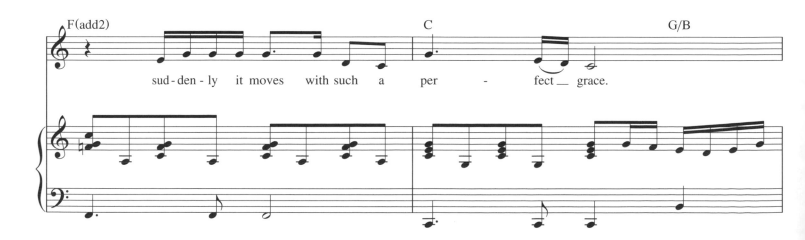

sud - den - ly it moves with such a per - fect _ grace.

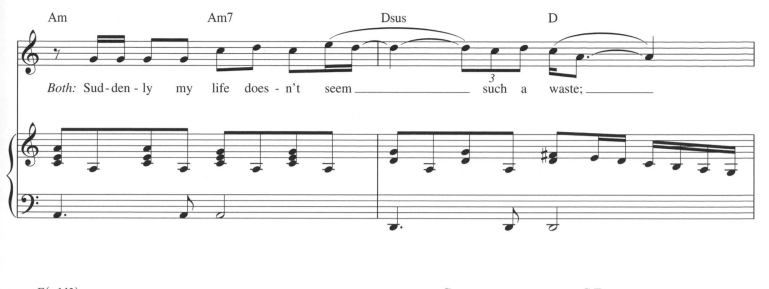

Both: Sud-den-ly my life does-n't seem _____ such a waste; _____

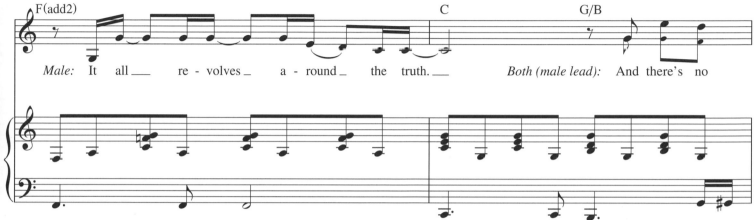

Male: It all ___ re- volves ___ a - round ___ the truth. ___ Both (male lead): And there's no

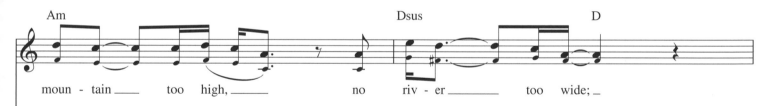

moun - tain ___ too high, _____ no riv - er _____ too wide; _

Male: sing out this song, _ and I'll be there _____ by your side. _
Female: sing out this song, _ and I'll be there _____ by your side. _

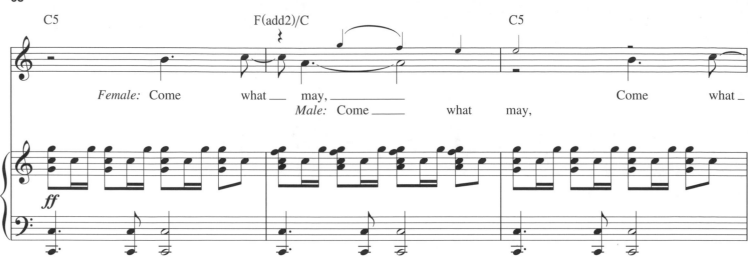

Female: Come what ___ may, ___ Come what ___
Male: Come ___ what may,

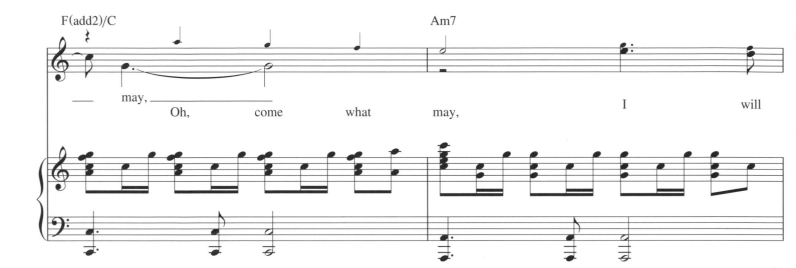

___ may, ___ I will
Oh, ___ come what may,

love you ___ un - til my dy - ing

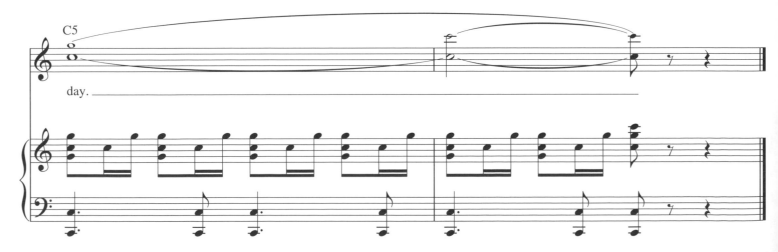

day. ___

SOME ENCHANTED EVENING
from SOUTH PACIFIC

Lyrics by OSCAR HAMMERSTEIN II
Music by RICHARD RODGERS

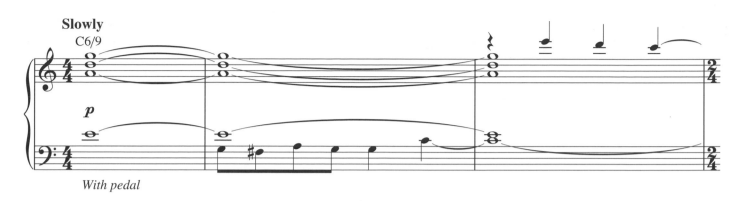

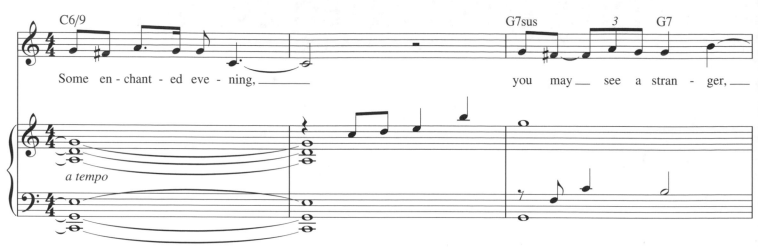

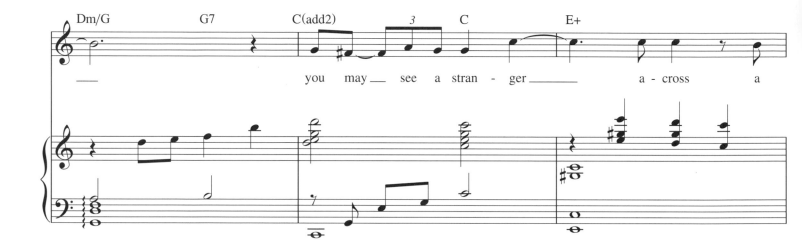

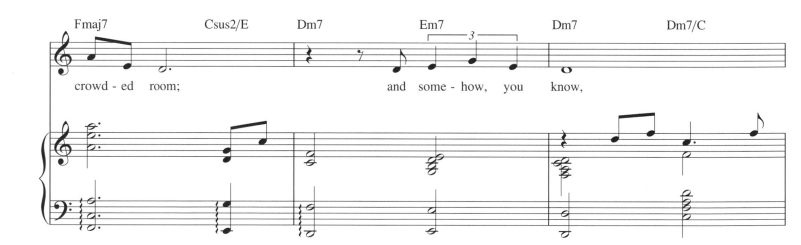

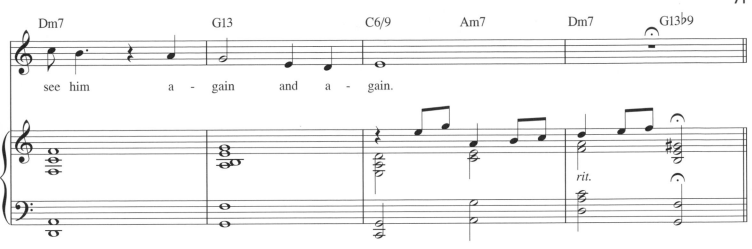

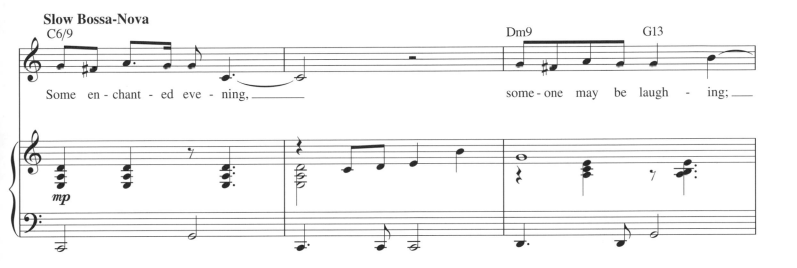

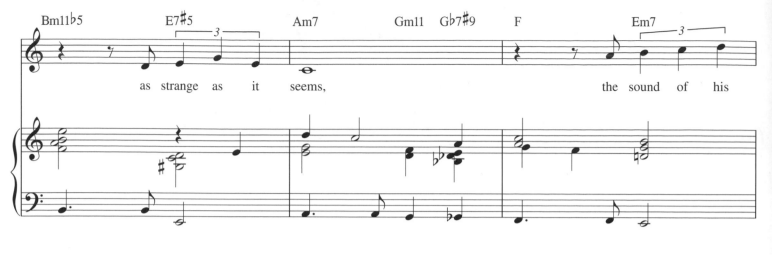

as strange as it seems, the sound of his

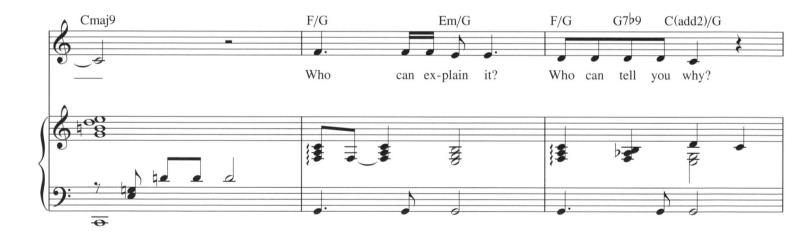

laugh - ter _____ will sing in your dreams. _____

Who can ex-plain it? Who can tell you why?

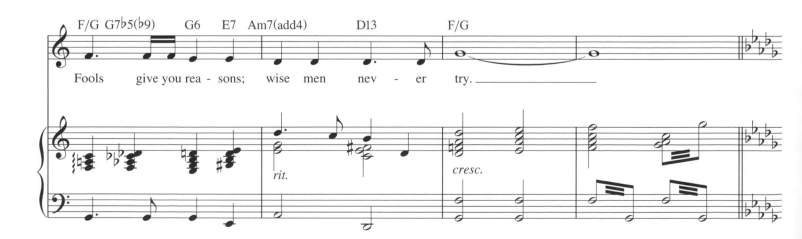

Fools give you rea - sons; wise men nev - er try. _____

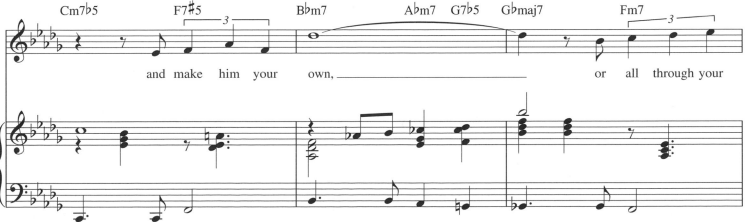

WHEN I FALL IN LOVE

featured in the TriStar Motion Picture SLEEPLESS IN SEATTLE

Words by EDWARD HEYMAN
Music by VICTOR YOUNG

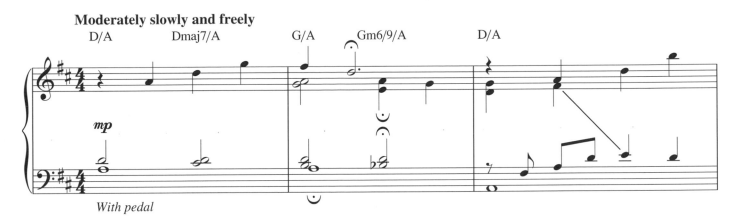

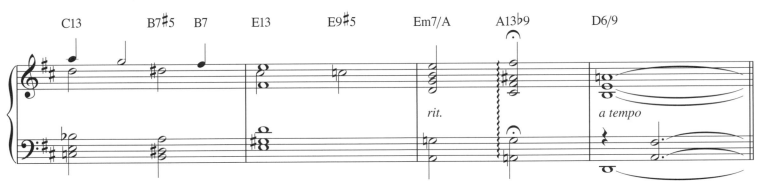

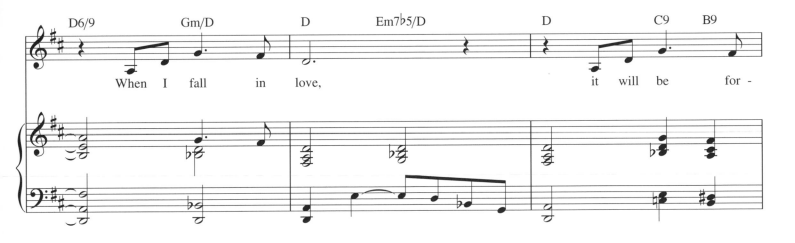

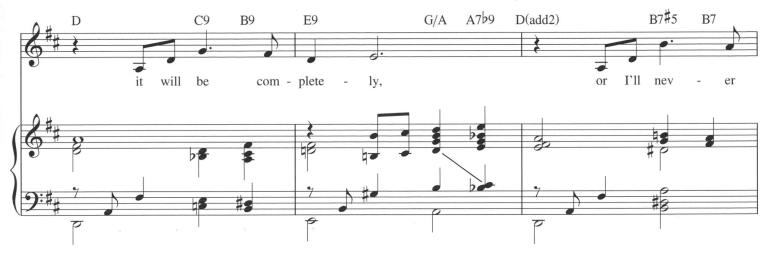

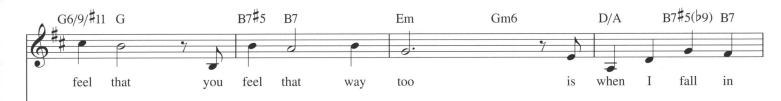

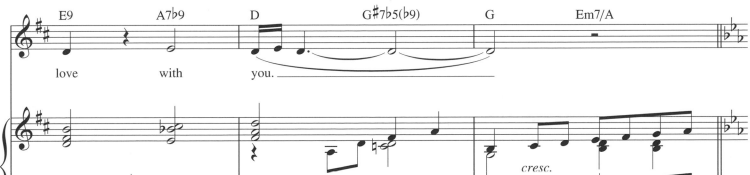

78

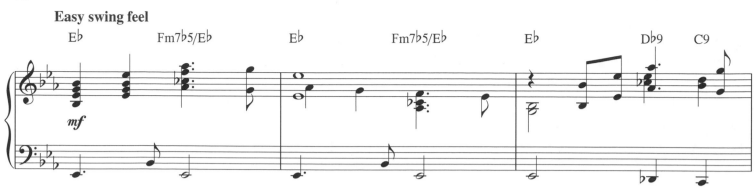

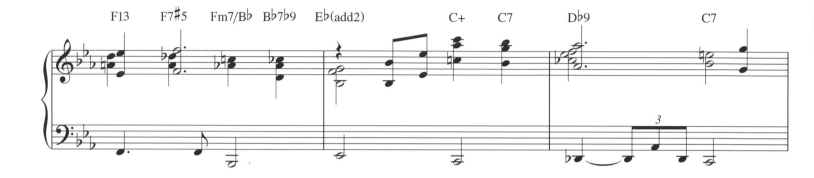

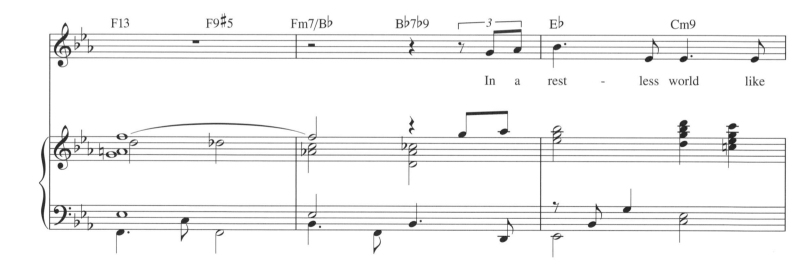

In a rest - less world like

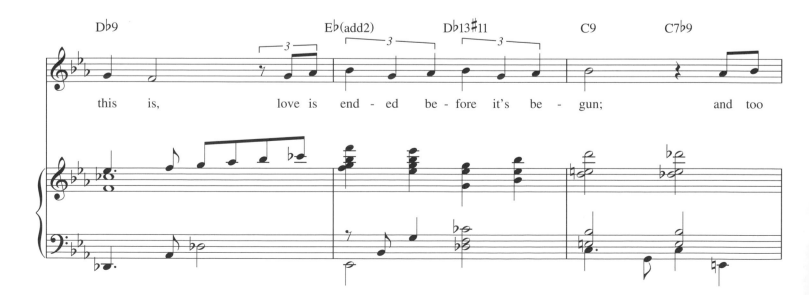

this is,   love is end - ed be - fore it's be - gun;   and too

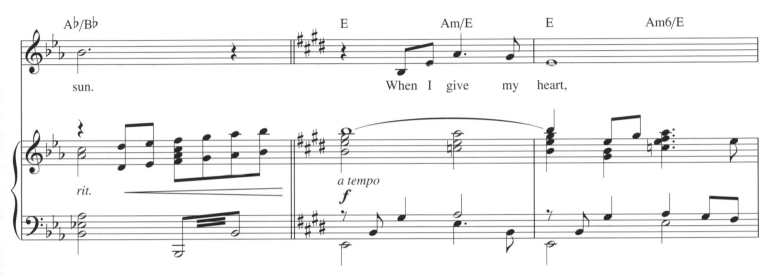

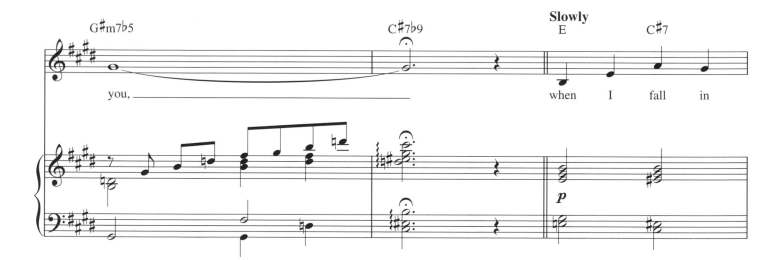

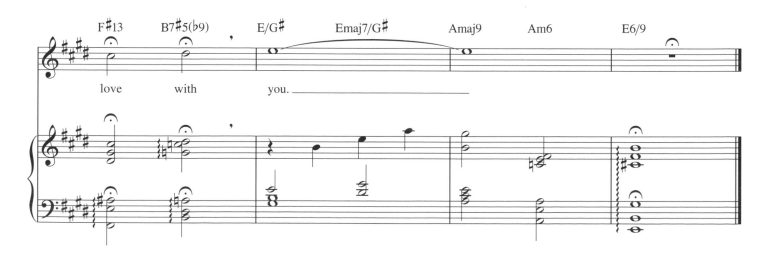